DRIVING
TEST *Tips*

Andrew Adams

D0434096

DRIVING TEST TIPS

First published in 2004
This edition copyright © Summersdale Publishers Ltd, 2014

Summersdale Publishers Ltd
46 West Street
Chichester
West Sussex
PO19 1RP
UK

www.summersdale.com

Printed and bound in the Czech Republic

ISBN: 978-1-84953-538-0

CONTENTS

Note: the information in this book refers mainly to those taking their driving test in the UK, in a regular car. Though the majority of the tips in this book can be applied to all kinds of driving tests, those looking for specific information for taking a test on a moped, motorbike, van, bus or lorry should check the gov.uk website for the most up-to-date information.

INTRODUCTION

You've been working hard at your lessons, mastering the gears and attempting to reverse your car around a corner smoothly for weeks, and now it's time to start thinking about the test itself. If you know the basics but are worried about the test, this book is what you need to overcome that anxiety.

You could have all the knowledge and driving skills necessary to pass your test but if nerves cause you to make a silly mistake it can all be wasted. Passing your driving test is as much about learning to take control of yourself as it is about taking control of your vehicle. It sounds a tall order but if you follow the tips in this book, try to relax and go into the test feeling calm and confident, you'll be on the road to success in no time.

THE THEORY TEST

Learning to drive is a complicated life skill, which can take many months to master. Every driver is different, and you should feel free to progress at your own pace during your lessons. Once you've built up the necessary basic skills, your instructor will start to prepare you for your theory test. The idea of the theory test is to check that you understand the essential rules of driving, can recognise and interpret road signs and have a good level of awareness, before you progress to the practical test. You need a theory test certificate before you can book a practical test.

OVERVIEW

The theory test is divided into two sections, which you'll take back to back (with a 3-minute interval in between) at an official test centre. The first is a multiple choice section, followed by a hazard perception section. You need to pass both parts in order to gain your theory test certificate. Whatever the outcome, you will receive your results at the end, and if you have been successful, you'll receive your certificate then and there – at least it's all over nice and quickly!

THE MULTIPLE CHOICE SECTION

The first part of the theory test consists of 50 multiple choice questions covering all aspects of driving, including some 'case studies' where you will be shown a short story about real-life driving experiences and then be asked five questions relating to it. You will be given the option to do a 'practice' session before you start, then you have 57 minutes to answer all the questions – the structured timing means that you should have enough time to think through each question carefully and then calm your nerves before moving on to the next one. To pass you need to answer 43 correctly.

THE HAZARD PERCEPTION SECTION

This is an electronic test of your awareness of potential hazards on the road. You will be shown a clip featuring an everyday scene, and asked to identify at least one 'developing hazard' per clip. This could be anything that might make you change your speed or direction, such as a car indicating to pull out, or a ball rolling into the road. You can score a maximum of five points per clip – the earlier you spot a hazard, the higher you will score. You have approximately 15 minutes to complete the test; the pass rate is 44 out of a possible 75.

PRACTISING FOR THE MULTIPLE CHOICE SECTION

The best way to prepare for the multiple choice part is to study the Highway Code in great detail, and to do as many mock theory tests as you can to test your knowledge. The gov.uk website has mock theory tests that you can do on the Internet, and there are various DVDs and books available with all the questions you're likely to be asked to practise with. You could also ask your friends and family to help you, testing you on the Highway Code.

PRACTISING FOR THE HAZARD PERCEPTION SECTION

There is an 'Official Guide to Hazard Perception' DVD, which offers comprehensive training for the test, but there are also mock tests available on the Internet, which make a great addition to these tools. They help you understand how they work and what to expect on the test day. It's particularly useful to analyse your score afterwards, so you can work out exactly what you need to do in order to achieve the highest possible results in the real thing.

WHERE AND WHEN TO STUDY

Find somewhere comfortable and quiet where you are unlikely to be disturbed to focus on studying the Highway Code. You may think parts of it seem obvious or that you can just pick it up as you go along, but there are lots of extra little details you will need to know during your theory test, so you need to be able to concentrate. You may find it more helpful to break up your study sessions and just focus on one small area of the Code at a time. It might also help to work out when you are at your most productive so that you can schedule your study periods for that time of day.

THE DAY OF THE TEST

Make sure you arrive at the test centre in plenty of time, so you are not rushed or stressed by delays. You need to bring both parts of your driving licence to the test centre (paper and photocard) or you will not be allowed to take the test. If you attempt to talk to or otherwise distract anybody, you will be asked to leave. You can't take any personal belongings into the test room either, so make sure you've put everything away in one of the lockers provided. Lastly – relax! The test is well structured and you should be well prepared by this point – you'll be fine.

PRACTISE AND PREPARE

Now the theory test is out of the way, it's time to focus on your driving skills and ways to prep yourself for the practical test.

TURN YOUR WEAKNESSES INTO STRENGTHS

Everyone has their weaknesses when it comes to learning to drive. It might be roundabouts, parking or changing gear smoothly. Don't overlook these problems: identify them and ask your instructor to help you work at them until they become your strongest skills.

TOP TIP

DON'T IGNORE ASPECTS OF DRIVING THAT YOU DON'T ENJOY

If you hate parallel parking, practise it until you can do it like a pro. Don't get a mental block about aspects of driving that you hate – just do it.

MASTER THE MANOEUVRES

Not knowing which manoeuvres you'll be asked to do or not feeling confident that you'll be able to do them can be the biggest cause of stress on the test day. Ask your instructor for clear rules to follow to make sure you get each of the main manoeuvres perfect each time.

PRACTISE IN ALL WEATHERS

An emergency stop on a dry road is very different to one in heavy rain. Since you won't be able to predict the weather on your test day make sure you're comfortable about driving in all weather conditions. An understanding of skid control will help if you have to stop suddenly in the wet.

UNDER THE BONNET

Part of the driving test includes testing your knowledge of basic car maintenance. You'll need to know how to check and top up oil, coolant, brake fluid and washer fluid for the 'show me, tell me' questions you'll have to answer on the day, so make sure your instructor talks you through this in your lessons until you are confident.

TYRES

You need to know how to check whether the tyres are at the correct pressure and have sufficient tread, and how to spot signs of damage that could make them unsafe for driving.

LIGHTS

Learn how to check that all the car's lights are working, including brake lights and indicators.

BRAKES

A demonstration that the brakes are in working order may be required before driving off in the test. Make sure your instructor shows you how to do this, plus how to test and look for signs of wear in the handbrake.

OTHER CAR FEATURES

Whatever your car offers by way of features, it's important to know how to operate them and how to check if they are not working. This includes the horn and power steering but doesn't apply to non-control items such as the stereo. It can also include heaters and demisters and you'll be expected to use them if appropriate.

BE FAMILIAR WITH YOUR CAR

All makes of car feel slightly different to drive, so don't change cars just before the test. The indicator lever might be on the other side of the steering wheel; the brakes might require more effort than you're used to; the switch for the lights might be somewhere different; the turning circle might be larger. It's important to be confident with your car and sticking with the same car you've learnt in (whether your own or your instructor's) is the only way to do that.

CHECK OUT THE SAFETY OF THE TEST CAR

If you're going to take the test in your own car rather than your instructor's, make sure it has a second rear-view mirror for the examiner to use. Also make sure it's clean and tidy and that the passenger seat belt functions correctly; the examiner won't come out on the test with you if there's anything wrong with it. You can check the exact requirements for a test car on the gov.uk website.

CHECK OUT THE LEGALITY OF THE TEST CAR

The tax disc, the insurance and the MOT must all be up to date. The speedometer must read in miles per hour. The examiner will refuse to go out in any car that isn't fully legal. Also check that your L-plates haven't fallen off and that they are clearly displayed.

DO A COUPLE OF MOCK TESTS

Your instructor will be able to take you through one or two mock tests, preferably starting and finishing at the site of the driving test centre. That way when it comes to the real thing you'll already know what it feels like to drive out of that car park and onto the road.

IF YOU FEEL COMFORTABLE, PRACTISE OUTSIDE OF YOUR LESSONS

As long as you have a provisional licence, you can practise driving with anyone who's over 21 and has had their licence for more than 3 years. This means you don't have to rely solely on your lessons – but do make sure you listen to your instructor's advice over that of your non-expert friends!

BOOKING YOUR PRACTICAL TEST

Only book your test when you and your instructor think you're ready. If you know you're not fully prepared you'll feel extra unnecessary stress, so make sure you don't take a test too soon.

MAKE THE DECISION

The driving test itself is not where you pass or fail. Although the test itself is the final hurdle, you'll already have done all the work needed to pass before the test. It's up to you to show the examiner that you deserve to pass.

PLAN AHEAD

Your driving test is a major landmark in your life. It's important to focus on it, so avoid booking a test that might coincide with other major life events such as exams, new babies, house moves, weddings, etc.

KEEP THE DAY CLEAR

Once you've set the date, make sure you don't fill the days preceding it with social events. Keep the day itself empty of appointments or engagements – that way you will not be distracted or stressed by delays during the test, and your mind will be completely focused.

TOP TIP

BOOK A MORNING TEST IF POSSIBLE

Many people find it easier to concentrate in the morning, before they get tired later in the day, so it may be a good idea to book a morning appointment if you can. It also means you won't spend all day worrying about the upcoming test, but make sure you factor in time to go through your usual morning routine without feeling stressed.

DON'T ANNOUNCE THE TEST DATE TO THE WORLD

If you feel pressured by having everyone giving you advice and recalling their own driving test nightmare experiences, don't tell them. If you pass you'll have a great surprise for them, and if you don't, you need only tell the people you want to know.

BANISH THOSE NERVES!

A state of nervousness is the body's evolved reaction to danger. It creates a change in a person's biochemical balance that enables a short-term enhancement of strength and senses designed to either get that person out of danger quickly by running, or to help them fight. Feeling nervous will help you, provided you don't let your worries get out of control.

RELISH THE NERVES

Being a little nervous puts your body in a slightly hyper state, fuelled by adrenalin that heightens your concentration and performance. Lots of performers use the power of the 'fight or flight' mechanism to achieve great heights in their work, so don't be scared of the feeling – harness it and use it to your advantage.

KEEP AN EYE ON STRESS

Don't ignore worries about your driving test. Stress can build up as multiple factors combine until you can't cope any more, so try to deal with every problem as it occurs so that the stress is always manageable. This also applies to the stresses of everyday life – keep them under control and you'll find you can cope with your driving test too.

EAT THE RIGHT THINGS

A balanced diet of natural and healthy foods will help your body to cope with stress more easily. Too much sugar or caffeine will exacerbate any feelings of stress you may have.

EAT CHOCOLATE

Despite chocolate's high sugar content there are a multitude of benefits to eating a few squares of dark chocolate every day. Studies suggest that dark chocolate can relieve stress and anxiety, improve mood and cognitive function and even create a sense of peace and relaxation.

DON'T CHANGE YOUR DIET AT THE LAST MINUTE

Suddenly switching to a new kind of diet, such as fat- or carbohydrate-free, just a few days before the driving test can unnecessarily complicate your body's ability to cope with stress.

WIND DOWN AT NIGHT

If the looming test day leaves you anxious last thing at night try to wind down with a hot bath or some soothing music.

BE PREPARED FOR BROKEN SLEEP

If you can't sleep well then don't fight it. Getting worked up about a sleepless night only makes it harder to sleep and leaves you more exhausted the next morning. It's normal to have broken sleep patterns when a challenging event such as a driving test approaches, so plan for this and try to find ways to minimise light and noise pollution in your bedroom to help you sleep. Drinking warm milk may help, too, as studies suggest that this reduces gastric secretion, influences stomach receptors and has a sedative effect.

DON'T CHEAT
YOUR BODY

You might think pills are a good way to calm the nerves, but they can impair concentration and slow your reaction times. Drinking heavily the night before the test in order to relax will also not help the next day. What's more, you could still have alcohol in your system when you come to take the test and therefore have a blood-alcohol level over the legal limit. Your body needs to be fresh and alert, not drugged-up and dazed.

AVOID SMOKING

Some people smoke to alleviate stress, but it also increases blood pressure and can add to feelings of anxiety. If you are looking to quit, seek advice from your doctor or a local stop smoking service.

TOP TIP

BREATHE

If the looming test date causes
anxiety, try this breathing technique.
It's simple, but surprisingly effective:
breathe in deep, hold for a few
seconds, breathe out. Repeat
several times, and focus on nothing
but your breathing. It helps to empty
your mind of worries and calms
your heart rate.

BELIEVE IN YOURSELF

You can do it. You've worked hard for this. You know how to drive. Think of a couple of particularly good lessons you've had recently, and take pleasure in the thought of showing off your skills to your examiner.

REMIND YOURSELF THAT YOU HAVE PASSED OTHER EXAMS IN YOUR LIFE

A driving test is an exam like any other. You've taken and passed exams that are much tougher than the driving test – don't forget that.

REMEMBER, THE EXAMINER IS HUMAN

They understand that you're nervous. They know the test means a lot to you. Within reason they will make allowances for this, especially in the first minute or so, provided your nervousness doesn't compromise safety.

MEDITATE

Find 5 minutes each day in the week before the test to sit in a quiet place, close your eyes, and let your mind take you to place of calm and serenity; perhaps a beach where the waves are lapping at your toes and the sun is warming your body. This will help to prevent a build-up of pre-test nerves.

RELAX YOUR MUSCLES

Muscle tension caused by stress can be alleviated by the simple technique of tensing and then relaxing each part of your body, one at a time, working from your toes up to your shoulders, then down your arms to your hands, and feeling the stress flowing out of you as you do so.

THE DAY OF THE TEST

The big day has arrived – time to put all those lessons into practice.

GET PLENTY OF SLEEP THE NIGHT BEFORE

Make time to relax the night before the test. Exercising in the early evening will help you to feel tired, making sure you get a good night's sleep so your concentration levels are as high as possible in the morning. Some candidates use energy drinks and tablets to compensate for lack of sleep, but high caffeine doses won't give you the same mental awareness as a good night's sleep.

TOP TIP

TAKE A SHOWER

Make yourself clean and presentable so you'll arrive for the test feeling fresh and awake. A brisk shower will energise you for the day ahead, and the better you feel about yourself, the more confident you'll be in the test.

EAT SOMETHING

Some people might feel too nervous to eat a good breakfast, but getting some food inside you will boost your concentration levels and give you the energy you need to keep you alert throughout the test. Good brain foods include eggs, yogurt, wholegrain cereal, fruit and nuts. If your test is later in the day, try filling up on blueberries, figs, carrots, spinach, cottage cheese and bananas. Don't force down food just before dashing off to the test though – a heavy meal can make you feel groggy for up to an hour after you eat it.

WEAR A WATCH

You don't want to be late for the test. There's no flexibility – if you miss your slot you'll have to book and pay for another test. Make sure you arrive at the test centre early.

REMEMBER THE DOCUMENTS

You'll need to bring your theory test pass certificate and both parts of your driving licence (paper and photocard) in order to be able to take the test. Your instructor will confirm the current legal requirements, or you can check on the gov.uk website.

HAVE A POSITIVE ATTITUDE

Start the day with a positive mental approach, telling yourself this is going to be the day that you pass your driving test and looking forward to the celebrations that will follow. For some people, it may help to visualise a worst-case scenario – this can help take the pressure off, as you realise that all that could happen is you might have to take the test again another day. Millions of people have retaken their test and gone on to pass, and there's no rule that says you have to pass first time.

REHEARSE IN YOUR HEAD

Take a moment to sit and go through some likely scenarios in your head. Picture yourself driving smoothly and confidently. Imagine feeling relaxed and listening attentively to the examiner's instructions whilst remaining focused on the road ahead and the vehicles around you.

TOP TIP

THINK AHEAD

One day you'll be an experienced driver. You'll drive every day without giving it a second thought. You'll be listening to the radio and thinking about what's for dinner, and all those parts of driving that now seem so complicated will be second nature to you. Try to picture yourself driving with that much confidence and take that confidence with you into the test.

VISUALISE SUCCESS

Lots of students spend their time pessimistically visualising failure, but experiments have shown that students who visualise themselves succeeding are more likely to succeed than those who don't. Imagine the scenario as your examiner tells you the good news – you've passed!

RATIONALISE

It's not rocket science: millions of people have already passed the test you are about to take. It was important to every one of them, just like it is to you, but they all managed to get through it – you can be one of them!

WARM UP WITH A MOCK DRIVING TEST BEFORE THE REAL ONE

Your driving instructor should take you round 'the course' (or at least the local area if you're not sure of an exact route) just before you do the real test so that the area feels familiar and you're fully in tune with your car and the roads.

WHAT TO WEAR

Choosing your outfit for the day carefully can have benefits in more ways than one. For example, choose comfort over style – no examiner will pass you because you have good dress sense. Dress for comfort and practicality rather than fashion.

SELECT THE RIGHT SHOES

Flat shoes or low-heeled shoes tend to be more practical for driving. If your shoes are so broad that it's hard to hit the brake pedal without hitting one of the other pedals at the same time, or if your stilettos don't give you the ankle leverage you need to depress the clutch fully, you're going to have problems. While it is not illegal to drive in unsuitable shoes, you have a responsibility as a road user to make sure you can retain absolute control of your vehicle at all times. Lightweight trainers are usually the best option: the rubber soles give good grip on the pedals. Whatever you choose, try to make sure you wear the same shoes you wore in your lessons so that you're used to how they feel on the pedals.

KEEP YOUR SHOES ON

Some people like to drive with no shoes at all, enjoying the feel of the pedals on bare feet. Although it's important to feel the pedals, shoes give the extra power to the feet that's needed in emergency braking situations – you just don't have as much braking force with bare feet as you would with shoes on.

IF YOU NEED GLASSES, WEAR THEM

If you need glasses to drive, it's a legal requirement that you make sure they are in good condition and wear them whenever you drive. If you fail the eyesight test you won't even get to drive out of the car park.

DURING THE TEST

Once you've registered your arrival at the test centre, you'll be introduced to your examiner who will conduct an eye test and lead you to your vehicle.

COME PREPARED

Before you drive off you will have to answer two 'show me, tell me' questions about vehicle safety and maintenance. It's an automatic fail if you get them wrong; make sure the answers are fresh in your mind so that you can show off your comprehensive knowledge to the examiner.

CHECK THE SEAT POSITION

Make sure the seat is in the right position for you to operate the controls comfortably and that the mirrors are correctly set.

START IT RIGHT

Gearstick in neutral, handbrake on. Even if you know they're in those positions, demonstrate to the examiner that you're checking. Remember to check all your mirrors before pulling away.

AIM FOR COMPETENCE NOT PERFECTION

The examiner is looking for a safe, competent driver. You don't have to be perfect. Small mistakes won't necessarily fail you so long as they don't represent a safety risk, so don't fixate on any small hiccups during the test.

TOP TIP

LISTEN

Listen to what your examiner is telling you to do. If you don't understand an instruction, don't be afraid to ask for clarification. Did they mean to turn left or to take the left lane? It is always far better to ask than to guess wrong and end up with a fail.

EXPLAIN YOURSELF

If you find yourself in a situation where the road conditions are forcing you to do something contrary to the examiner's instructions, such as failing to get into the appropriate lane due to density of traffic, just explain what you're doing and why, and propose an alternative.

DON'T GIVE UP

If you think you've made a mistake that will result in failure, don't give up. Accept it, relax and keep driving until the test is over. It's always possible that the examiner either didn't notice the mistake or didn't plan to fail you because of it. Correct your own mistakes quickly – if you change to the wrong gear, fix it immediately. If you stall, calmly enter the stall drill straight away without sighing or cursing.

RELAX, THE DRIVING LICENCE IS (ALMOST) YOURS FOR THE TAKING

The examiner won't fail you just because he passed the previous two people. You will pass if you drive in a manner that demonstrates you're safe to be let loose on the roads. It's up to you to show that; convince the examiner with your competence and the driving licence is in the bag.

KEEP IT SMOOTH

Part of demonstrating your competence in the car is to give a smooth ride for the examiner. You should be aiming to drive so that if there was a glass of water on the dashboard, you wouldn't spill a drop. This means smooth gear changes, the right speed around corners, braking progressively and in good time and not hitting anything!

DON'T COPY BAD HABITS

You'll see bad behaviour on the roads, but don't be tempted to copy it. Ignore any pressure from other drivers and remember that their actions aren't being watched – yours are. If you are a victim of road rage, don't react in a similar manner; the examiner may be sympathetic to you as a person, but will still mark you down for any poor conduct.

ANTICIPATE

Look out for signs of potential hazards ahead. Your examiner will be checking to see that you anticipate that a car is about to pull out in front of you or a pedestrian is about to cross the road. Observing people and cars ahead (both stationary and moving) is a matter of common sense. For instance, a smoky-looking exhaust from a parked car on a cold day is a sign that the engine's just been turned on and the driver is likely to be about to pull out; children playing football near the road could suddenly kick the ball into the street and run after it, etc.

DEMONSTRATE FULL AWARENESS OF THE ROAD AROUND YOU

That means what's ahead of you and what's behind. Using mirrors correctly will show that you're aware of surrounding traffic – make sure you always use the rear-view mirror before applying the brakes, unless it's an emergency stop, and before you indicate.

TOP TIP

PACE YOURSELF

Don't be forced into sudden evasive manoeuvres by not thinking ahead. Your driving and your thinking should be at a steady pace – don't let your thinking lag behind or your driving race ahead of your ability to control it!

PREPARE FOR THE UNEXPECTED

Anything could happen on the test and part of your job as a driver is to demonstrate your ability to cope with real-world situations that arise. If you face a situation you've not encountered before, such as a police roadblock or an unexpected diversion, try not to panic. Look at what the other cars around you are doing. Follow instructions from your examiner or the police, if appropriate. Take your time to understand the situation, and look at the options open to you before making a decision.

ACCEPT THINGS YOU CANNOT CHANGE

If the weather takes a turn for the worse during your test, or you come across unexpected road works or traffic, try not to worry. You can't change these things, but you can react as gracefully as possible and make all the right decisions, based on what you've learnt in your lessons.

REMEMBER: SILENCE MEANS GO STRAIGHT

If the examiner doesn't give you any instructions for a while, you should assume you're meant to keep going. Therefore at a crossroads or a mini-roundabout go straight over. Choose the appropriate lane for continuing on the same route when faced with a choice and no instructions.

BE AWARE AT ROUNDABOUTS

Concentrate on the road signs as well as the instructions from the examiner. For some roundabouts the instruction 'take the second exit' requires you to be in the left lane, for others you might need to be in the right lane and on some you have a choice. Make sure you're aware of the position of your exit relative to your start position on the roundabout.

USE THE HANDBRAKE APPROPRIATELY

Always use the handbrake if stopping on a hill or for more than a couple of seconds, but not indiscriminately at every pause in the traffic. You may think using the handbrake is an unnecessary hassle, but there are important reasons this rule is enforced – firstly, if another road user drives into the back of your car, the handbrake will prevent your car from flying out into the course of oncoming traffic; and secondly, releasing the footbrake deactivates the brake lights, which means there's less glare for the road users behind you.

TAKE THE NEXT AVAILABLE TURN

When instructed to turn into the next available road, make sure you're aware of any 'unavailable' roads that might come first, such as no-entry roads. Your examiner expects you to have the common sense to take the next turn that is actually legal. If you feel the instruction is ambiguous because there's a small road coming up that you think might be a private drive or a car park entrance instead of a proper junction, just ask for clarification.

TAKE EXTRA CARE MOVING TO THE RIGHT

It's always possible that someone may try to overtake you, so a final check before turning right or changing lanes to the right is essential. This also applies when changing lanes to the left – even though no one is meant to overtake you on the inside, that doesn't mean they won't try. Even if the other car is breaking the law you'll fail your test if you don't spot them whizzing past you in the inside lane.

CONTROL THE CAR WITH CONFIDENCE

Use the gears as they are intended. If you stay in a low gear at high speed, even for a short distance, it's a sign of being a nervous driver (and it's not good for the car's engine either), so don't be afraid to change gear as often as is necessary.

DRIVE AT THE RIGHT SPEED FOR THE ROAD

Speed limits can change unexpectedly and often, so demonstrate to your examiner that you're aware of these different limits by speeding up where appropriate and safe to do so and slowing down before entering lower-limit areas.

TOP TIP

DRIVE AT THE RIGHT SPEED FOR THE CONDITIONS

Don't treat the speed limit as a target – if it isn't safe to drive at 60 mph on a 60-mph road, don't. Reasons it may not be safe include bad weather, poor visibility, lots of pedestrians or extra traffic (e.g. around a fete or festival), road works and diversions.

KEEP YOUR EYE ON THE ROAD

Most of your car's controls are designed to be used without the driver having to look at them. You should be able to use the foot pedals, change gear and indicate without taking an eye off the road.

LISTEN OUT

The sounds of the road can also help you in making judgements, so make sure you're listening attentively while you drive so you can react appropriately – not just to your examiner, but also for signs such as police or ambulance sirens (you should pull in if safe to do so to let them pass), car horns going off ahead (which could suggest you're approaching a traffic jam or an accident), and the sound of cars approaching if you're waiting to pull out at a junction and your visibility is limited.

DON'T SHOW OFF TOO MUCH

Proudly display your regular driving skills, but don't show off in the same way you might be tempted to in order to give your friends a thrill when driving them. You may be confident that you can get the car through a tight gap between other vehicles, but if you charge through that gap so fast that you frighten the examiner they are likely to mark you down for it, if not give you an automatic fail. You should be showing you can drive *safely*, not impressively.

PASS OR FAIL?

In order to pass your test, you must have made no more than 15 driving faults, with no serious or dangerous faults. At the end of the test, the examiner will tell you whether or not you have passed and offer feedback to explain how you did. If you like, you can call your instructor over at this point to listen to the examiner's feedback so that, if you do fail, they will know what needs work.

DRIVING FAULTS (MINOR)

The most common errors made in a driving test are often the small ones. Though they are not enough on their own to warrant a fail, it doesn't mean you shouldn't pay attention to them – collect too many minor faults (currently 16) and you'll be failed. The examiner will classify the fault as a minor one if it doesn't represent a direct safety hazard (such as crunching the gears or stalling at a junction). If you make the same fault throughout your test it could become a serious fault.

SERIOUS FAULTS

If a fault is judged to be serious, then the whole test will be failed. A serious fault is one that has the potential to be dangerous but doesn't involve a third party. Failing two 'show me, tell me' questions prior to the driving part of the test also constitutes a serious fault.

DANGEROUS FAULTS

These are often instances when the examiner has to intervene to prevent an accident, either by giving you verbal instructions or trying to take control of the car. A dangerous fault means instant failure. If another road user has to swerve to avoid you, if there is danger to you, the examiner, the public or property, if you have an accident or if the examiner feels you have executed a dangerous manoeuvre then you will fail.

WHY PEOPLE FAIL

It can be useful to familiarise yourself with the main causes of failure, so you can identify whether you are likely to suffer from any weak spots you may have. If so, you should spend extra time working on these things in the lead-up to your test to make sure you're confident enough to avoid any of these pitfalls.

JUNCTIONS

One of the most common reasons people fail is because they don't know how to negotiate junctions. This covers roundabouts, traffic lights, crossroads and other junctions, and can involve failure to indicate correctly, taking the wrong lane and taking the turn in a less than safe and legal manner.

REVERSING ROUND A CORNER

This is a skill that takes practice and development of spatial awareness. Remember to ask your instructor for tips and keep at it in your lessons until you get it right every time.

STEERING

Another common cause of test failure is incorrect steering. This includes the way you hold and turn the wheel and your skill at keeping the vehicle safely on the road and in its lane while cornering and turning.

PARKING

Always near the top of the list of reasons for failure is reverse parking. Practice is the only way to make sure that both your parallel and bay parking is good enough to pass.

GEARS

Incorrect use of the gears also frequently appears on reasons for failure. Your choice of gear should be instinctive by the time you take the test. If you're still having to think about which gear is appropriate then you haven't done enough driving.

MIRRORS

Improper use of the mirror is next on the list of failure reasons. Usually it's due to not looking in the mirror when necessary, or looking during or after a manoeuvre instead of before. It can also be for failing to act on what is seen in the mirror; it's no use looking in the mirror if you don't take notice of what you see in it.

SPEED

Surprisingly, it's driving too slowly that fails more people than driving too fast. Don't drive like a nervous learner – drive like you know what you're doing and can cope on modern cut-throat busy roads. The only way to achieve this kind of confidence is to practise, practise and practise!

TURNING RIGHT

This manoeuvre is a sticking point for a lot of drivers. You need to know the rules of the road instinctively and you need to have had enough experience to be confident in applying those rules to the situation.

HESITANCY

If you pause too long when it's clearly safe to proceed at a junction then you're holding up traffic behind you and demonstrating that you're not yet a fully competent driver. Worse still, waiting too long to proceed sometimes means that you end up pulling out in front of approaching cars forcing them to slow down.

PULLING AWAY

Whether you're paused or parked, there are procedures for pulling away and joining the flow of traffic. Incorrect technique for this is high on the list of most common causes of failure.

EMERGENCY STOP

Skidding by braking too hard or failing to stop quickly enough by braking too softly won't convince the examiner that you can be relied upon to act safely if, for example, a child runs into the road.

STOPPING DISTANCE

If you let your concentration lapse and end up too close to the car in front then it's likely you'll fail.

ACCELERATOR

If used with a 'heavy right foot' then this pedal can fail you. Similarly, over-revving the engine through poor co-ordination with the clutch and generally displaying lack of competence with the pedals will result in failure.

CLUTCH

Whether it's riding the clutch (unnecessarily depressing the clutch when driving), inadequate depression leading to a stalled engine or a crunchy gear change, failure to show control of this pedal can mean failing the test.

FOOTBRAKE

Braking should be smooth and progressive, so that as your speed decreases the amount of pressure on the footbrake is reduced. This avoids sudden jolting stops. If the footbrake is used too late, too soon, too sharply or not at all, it can fail you.

HANDBRAKE

Usage before stopping, not releasing it before moving, not pulling it hard enough or not using it at all when you should can lead to failure. On hill starts, develop a sense of balance between the pull of the engine and the pull of the handbrake before releasing it.

STOP JUNCTIONS

These are different from normal 'give way' junctions for a reason: the view of the road is usually restricted and can only be observed once your vehicle is stationary. So make sure you stop completely before moving on even if the road is clear. Coasting towards the sign without stopping and then pulling straight onto the other road can be a cause of failure.

SIGNALS

The whole point of indicating is to help other road users anticipate your movements. If your signals are misleading, too early, too late or missing entirely, then it's a fail. It's best to indicate even if you don't see any other vehicles around, because there might be other road users that you didn't spot (such as pedestrians) who will base their decision as to when to cross the road on your signals.

NOT BEING READY

Some people take the test hoping for a fluke, knowing their driving skills are not consistently good enough to guarantee a pass. This usually results in failure.

OVERWHELMED BY STRESS

When stress can't be controlled it leads to panic. In that state of mind students perform very poorly, and can find themselves unable to concentrate. This can happen to people who can drive well in their lessons but who cannot cope with the pressure of the real test. Students often think more about the significance the test has to their future lives and careers than they do about the mechanics of actually passing it. Use the techniques given earlier in this book to help you manage your stress levels.

OVERCONFIDENCE

Eliminating all signs of test-related stress is generally a good thing, but if it makes you too confident of your skills or in denial of the reality of your state of preparedness then it can have a negative effect. Balance your confidence with respect for the road and for the examiner.

PRE-ASSUMPTION OF FAILURE

Pessimistic students do themselves no favours by assuming they will fail before they have even arrived at the test centre. This negative attitude reduces the chances of success, so remember to practise the positive visualisation techniques explained earlier.

SCARED EXAMINER

If the examiner thinks your driving style is putting them in danger, they can stop the test at any point and fail you on the spot. This is done for their protection and for that of other road users. Make sure that by the time you book your test, you are a confident and calm enough driver that you will put your examiner at ease.

YOU'RE NOT READY TO BANISH THOSE L-PLATES

You have to earn the right to remove the L-plates, and the test is your chance to demonstrate that you're ready. Driving is a complicated skill, and it's important that the examiner only passes those students who demonstrate total competence. Failing a student who isn't ready is fairer on both the student and other road users – it shouldn't be viewed negatively, but rather as a sign that you need to develop certain areas of your driving.

IF YOU FAIL

You will be told why you failed. Often it will be just one or two reasons. You may feel you were unfairly penalised if they seem like small errors, but this does at least mean that the rest of your driving was good enough and all you need to do is focus your next few lessons on the weak areas that have been identified.

TOP TIP

TAKE RESPONSIBILITY

An examiner wants you to demonstrate responsibility. A car is potentially dangerous and has to be driven responsibly. Think about whether you're really able to demonstrate adequate responsibility yet or whether you need to improve your vehicle control and knowledge.

IMPROVE YOUR CONFIDENCE

Don't take failure to heart. You need to improve your confidence, not allow it to take a knock. Build up your confidence at driving before taking the test again.

CHECK YOUR ATTITUDE

If you failed because your attitude showed aggression or lack of consideration towards other road users, including pedestrians, you need to look at your whole approach to driving. Do you see every other vehicle as an annoyance getting in your way? Do you feel everyone is out to stop you getting from A to B quickly enough? If so, remember that the roads don't belong to you. You've got to share them with everyone else, fast or slow. Accept it, deal with it and relax.

GOOD LUCK!

You've practised your 'show me, tell me' answers, you've flown through your mock tests and you've perfected your mirror, signal, manoeuvre technique – now it's time for the real thing. Remember, you've worked hard for this, and there's no reason you shouldn't be able to take off those L-plates as soon as you pull back in to the test centre. Stay calm, breathe deep, remember everything you've been taught, and you'll be fine. All that's left to do is go and celebrate when you pass!

If you're interested in finding out more about our books, find us on Facebook at **Summersdale Publishers** and follow us on Twitter at @Summersdale.

www.summersdale.com